Wild About Bears

Giant panda

Wild About

Asiatic black bear

Bears

Jeannie Brett

Charlesbridge

For my husband, Greg,
and our three bears:
Gregory, Sophie, and Lee;
and with special thanks to Yolanda

Many thanks to Shannon Donahue at the Great Bear
Foundation for all her help and support while
I was gathering facts for this book.

Published by Charlesbridge
85 Main Street
Watertown, MA 02472
(617) 926-0329
www.charlesbridge.com

Library of Congress Cataloging-in-Publication Data
Brett, Jeannie.
    Wild about bears / Jeannie Brett.
        pages cm
    Includes bibliographical references and index.
    ISBN 978-1-58089-418-0 (reinforced for library use)
    ISBN 978-1-58089-419-7 (softcover)
    ISBN 978-1-60734-636-4 (ebook)
1. Bears—Juvenile literature. I. Title.
QL737.C27B7327 2013
599.78—dc23   2012038700

Printed in Singapore
(hc) 10 9 8 7 6 5 4 3 2 1
(sc) 10 9 8 7 6 5 4 3 2 1

Illustrations done in watercolor on 300-lb. Arches hot-press paper
Display type and text type set in Museo Sans
Color separations by KHL Chroma Graphics, Singapore
Printed and bound September 2013 by Imago in Singapore
Production supervision by Brian G. Walker
Designed by Susan Mallory Sherman

Spectacled bear

Eight bear species

live on earth today: the polar bear, brown bear, North American black bear, spectacled bear, Asiatic black bear, sloth bear, sun bear, and giant panda. From the Arctic ice cap to South American cloud forests to the Tibetan plateau, the habitats of these bear species are as diverse as their traits and behaviors.

And yet wild bears have much in common, too. Often misunderstood or exploited, bears are curious creatures with unique qualities that make them an important part of the world's biodiversity.

Physical Traits

A bear's fur coat is adapted to the bear's habitat. Fur helps bears blend into their surroundings, repels water, and protects them from cold, heat, insects, branches, and dirt.

Bear cubs are nearly hairless, blind, and tiny at birth, weighing only 4–16 ounces. They grow quickly on a steady diet of nutritious mother's milk.

All bears are plantigrades—they walk with the entire soles of their feet on the ground, as humans do. They have five claws on each paw that cannot be pulled in the way a cat's can.

Bears are fast runners for short distances, clocking up to 35 miles per hour. That's as fast as a horse.

Bears have an astounding sense of smell. They use it to find mates, identify cubs, detect danger, locate food, and navigate.

Brown bear

Behavior

A bear's memory and sense of direction enable it to travel over 100 miles and still find its way back home.

Bears have day beds for resting. Spectacled bears, sun bears, Asiatic black bears, and sloth bears nap in trees. Polar bears rest in ice and snow. Giant pandas might use a hollow tree, a cave, or a bed of bamboo. Brown bears and North American black bears make beds of grass or conifer needles.

Many bears mark their home range by clawing and scratching tree trunks, rubbing against trees to leave a scent, and urinating near trees. This marking alerts other bears to their presence. It may also signal that a bear wants to mate.

Some northern bears hibernate, also called denning. They sleep through much of the winter to conserve energy when food is scarce.

Bears are omnivores and eat a variety of plants and animals. The giant panda is sometimes called an herbivore because of the large quantity of bamboo it consumes. Eating primarily seals, the polar bear is often referred to as a carnivore.

Sloth, spectacled, and sun bears are nocturnal, or active at night. Other bears are active during the day as well as at night.

North American black bear

Bear families consist of a sow (mother) and cubs (babies). The boar (father) leaves the child-rearing to the sow. Bear cubs stay with their mothers for one to three years. Mother bears are fierce protectors.

Polar bear

Ursus maritimus

Common names: sea bear, nanook, great white bear
Size: 400–1,600 pounds

The polar bear, a marine mammal, is the largest bear species. Its streamlined body makes it an expert swimmer. Polar bears eat ringed seals, kelp, berries, and grass. They live in the Arctic Circle.

A polar bear appears to have white fur, but its guard hairs, which excel at shedding water, are actually clear, hollow, and hard. A dense layer of underfur traps air next to the bear's skin, keeping it warm and dry. Its skin is black and absorbs heat from the sun. Polar bears have a thick layer of fat to keep them warm and buoyant.

Polar bears have partially webbed feet for swimming. The soles of their feet are covered with tiny suction cups called vacuoles, which give the bears excellent traction on ice and snow.

Only pregnant females hibernate in winter. In their ice dens, mother bears give birth to an average of two cubs.

Polar bears depend on the thick, stable sea ice of the Arctic ice cap for hunting, mating, denning, and traveling.

The grizzly bear gets its name from its silver-tipped hair, which makes it look streaked with gray, or "grizzly."

Brown bear

Ursus arctos

Common names: grizzly bear, coastal brown bear, Russian brown bear
Size: 200–1,000 pounds

Cubs are born in the mother bear's den during the winter months. There are usually one to four cubs in a litter.

Brown bears are usually medium brown, but their color can vary from blond to black and sometimes white. The Kodiak bear, a subspecies of the brown bear, is found only on Alaska's Kodiak Island.

The brown bear's slightly curved claws, which grow up to four inches long, are perfect for digging up roots and insects.

Brown bears live in mountain meadows, forests, and grasslands. They roam up to one thousand square miles, the largest home range of any land mammal. When food is abundant, they might stay in a ten- to twenty-mile range.

North American black bear

Ursus americanus

Common name: black bear
Size: 100–500 pounds

The North American black bear varies in color from black to brown to cinnamon. The rare glacier bear, a subspecies, has a bluish-gray coat, and the Kermode, or spirit bear, can be white.

North American black bears have sharp, curved claws about two inches long, which are helpful for a quick climb up a nearby tree.

These highly adaptable bears are the most common bears in the world today. They live in a wide variety of habitats, including forests, low-elevation swamps, and high mountain meadows.

One litter may contain different colored cubs.

Cubs climb trees for protection from predators.

Spectacled bears have thirteen pairs of ribs, while the other bear species have fourteen.

Each bear's markings are unique, just like human fingerprints.

Spectacled bear

Tremarctos ornatus

Common name: Andean bear
Size: 140–385 pounds

Bromeliads, a type of plant, are among the spectacled bear's favorite meals.

The spectacled bear gets its name from the cream-colored rings of fur around its eyes, which can make it look as if it is wearing glasses.

Spectacled bears spend a lot of time in trees. They make crude nests from bent and broken branches. These nests give them easy access to favorite plant foods and also serve as a lookout.

The spectacled bear lives in foggy, humid cloud forests at high elevations but may also be found in coastal and inland deserts, dry forests, rain forests, steppes, and plateaus.

Asiatic black bear

Ursus thibetanus

Common names: Himalayan black bear, Japanese black bear, Tibetan moon bear

Size: 110–440 pounds

The jet-black Asiatic black bear is often referred to as the Tibetan moon bear because of the white, crescent-shaped marking on its chest. Asiatic black bears like hilly or mountainous forest areas, from coastal foothills up to elevations of thirteen thousand feet. This adaptable bear is at home in trees, where it builds simple nests and platforms.

Asiatic black bears sometimes prey on livestock and damage valuable timber trees, which often causes conflict with humans. They also eat beetle larvae, termites, and honey.

Asiatic black bear nests look a lot like large bird nests and may be found 60 feet up in a tree.

Asiatic black bears use their short, strong claws for opening termite mounds and peeling off tree bark to eat the soft wood underneath.

Sloth bear

Ursus ursinus

Common name: honey bear
Size: 120–310 pounds

The shy, slow-moving sloth bear often hangs from tree limbs, like the sloth for which it is named. Sloth bears live in a variety of habitats, from grasslands to rocky outcrops to dry thorn forests and rain forests. They share their habitat with tigers and may scavenge from tigers' kills.

The sloth bear's favorite foods are termites and ants. It sniffs out insect colonies and digs out the mounds with its three-inch claws. The bear then blows the dirt away with its flexible lips. The roof of its mouth is arched, and it has no top front teeth—it can slurp up the insect treat with ease.

Sloth bear cubs often catch a ride on their mother's back, clinging to her shaggy fur.

The sucking noise of the sloth bear's snout can be heard from 300 feet away.

Sun bear

Ursus malayanus

Common name: dog bear, honey bear, Malayan sun bear
Size: 60–145 pounds

The reclusive sun bear is the smallest and least studied of the eight bear species. It lives in hot and humid rain forests. Its extra-long tongue helps it feed on honey and bee larvae. The sun bear's diet can also include snails, eggs, and lizards.

The long, curved claws and bowed legs of the sun bear make it an excellent tree climber. It spends its days sleeping and sunbathing high among the tree branches.

The sun bear's thick, short fur protects it from insect bites, twigs, dirt, and mud.

The sun bear has bare-soled paws that give it extra grip when climbing.

Giant panda

Ailuropoda melanoleuca

Common name: panda
Size: 155–275 pounds

This black-and-white bear is the rarest of the world's bears, with an estimated 1,000 to 2,500 giant pandas remaining in the wild. With its distinctive markings, the giant panda has become a worldwide symbol for conservation.

Most of the world's giant pandas live in fourteen nature reserves established along the eastern rim of the Tibetan plateau. Giant pandas like to live in cold, damp coniferous forests at high elevations.

The giant panda eats twenty-six to thirty-three pounds of bamboo every day. The need for large amounts of bamboo makes the giant panda less adaptable to its changing world.

Unlike other bear species, the giant panda does not have heel pads on its rear feet.

Giant panda cubs are born white and develop their black coloring later. They weigh only 4 ounces at birth.

Giant pandas have enlarged flexible wrists that act like an opposable thumb or a sixth digit.

Bears around the world

face many challenges. The destruction of forests, oil and gas extraction, and climate change threaten bears and their habitats. Poaching, the illegal bear parts trade, and the Eastern medicinal market threaten bears' survival as well.

Educating people about bears and preserving bear habitats around the world saves not only wild bears but also the entire ecosystem in which they live. The world's eight great species of bears will continue to inspire and fascinate us as long as we do our part to protect and preserve their way of life.

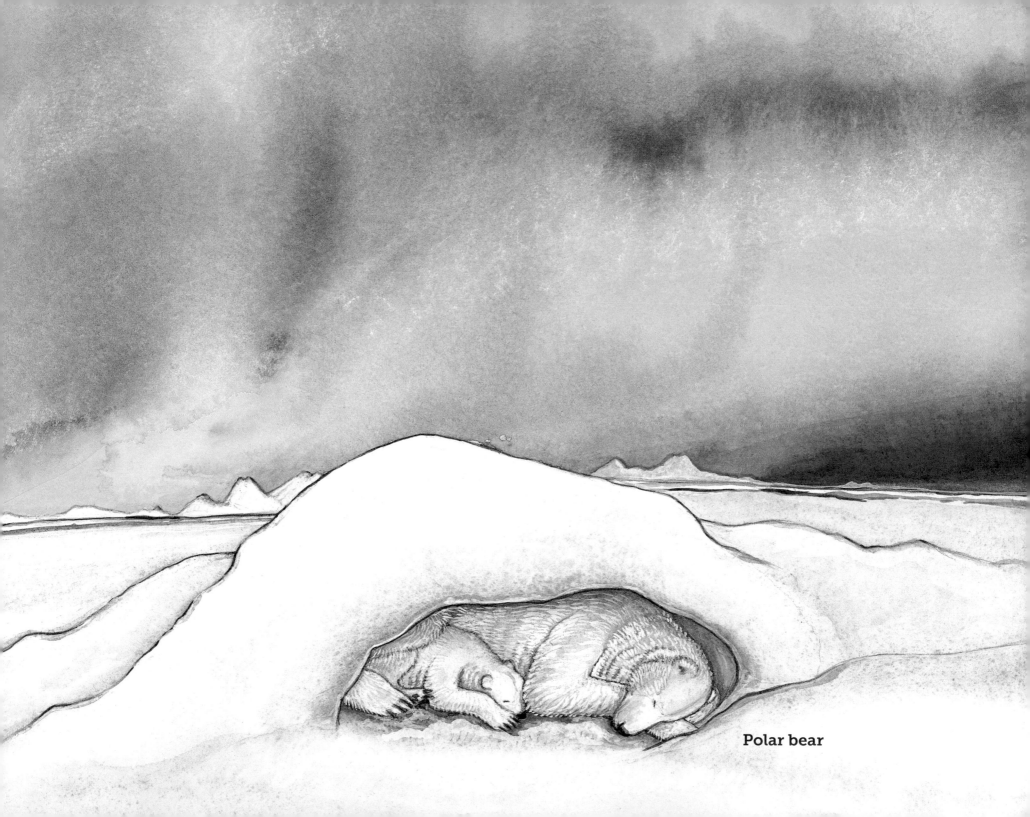

Polar bear

Where Bears Live

- Polar bear
- Brown bear
- North American black bear
- Spectacled bear
- Asiatic black bear
- Sloth bear
- Sun bear
- Giant panda

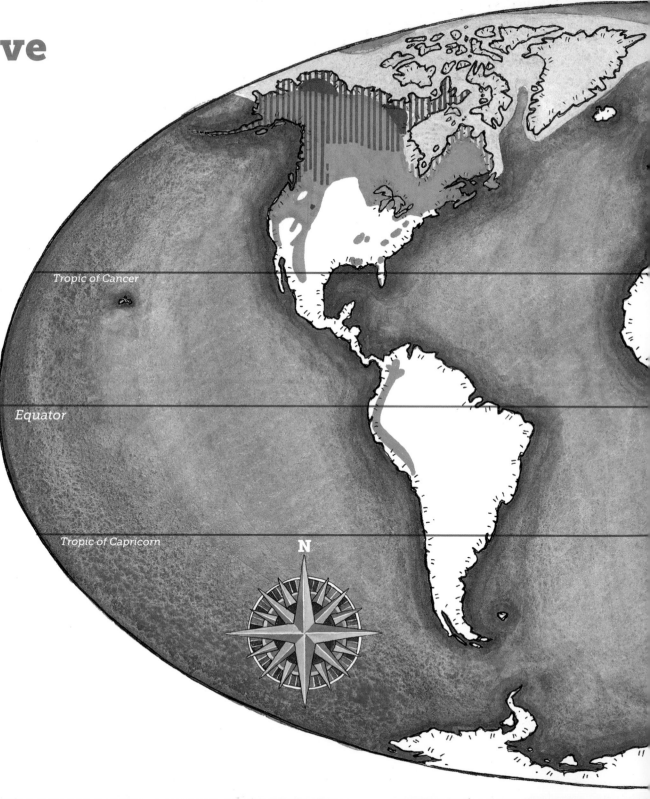

Tropic of Cancer

Equator

Tropic of Capricorn

N